D1088190

Building
without
Barriers

for the
Disabled

/Building without Barriers

for the Disabled /

Sarah P. Harkness
James N. Groom, Jr.

The Architects
Collaborative Inc.
Cambridge
Massachusetts

WHITNEY LIBRARY OF DESIGN
an imprint of
WATSON-GUPTILL PUBLICATIONS
New York

Library of Congress Cataloging in Publication Data
Harkness, Sarah P.   1914–
    Building without barriers for the disabled.
    Bibliography: p.
    Includes index.
    I. Architecture and the physically handicapped.
I. Groom, James N., 1941– joint author.
II. Title.
NA2545 . P5H37   720   76-20691
ISBN 0-8230-7082-4

First Printing, 1976

Second Printing, 1977

Traditionally, architects plan buildings with a certain population in mind. That population assumes abilities, needs, desires, capabilities, and tastes similar to those of the architect. There is usually a lack of empathy for anyone with differing characteristics because the user is, in fact, a figment of the architect's imagination.

Consider a concept of design where the user is not known, but every possibility is accommodated. The architect may not be pregnant today, but she or a friend may become so. The planner may not have a broken leg today, but he or his father may soon fall down a flight of steps. The designer may not be in a wheelchair today, but tomorrow he or she could be in a car accident and confined to one for life. Why not plan for every possibility so the environment can continue to be as convenient, functional, efficient, and usable as it was originally conceived? This is the concept of barrier-free design. It is not "special," it is not "traditional," it is human.

This book provides information on methods of designing to accommodate some of the possible circumstances people may face. Though it includes specifics on design features needed by the physically handicapped, keep in mind that these are features which will save every user time and energy in a safer environment.

The criteria are not "special." They are guidelines for an environment void of inconvenient elements requiring us to adapt, an environment which is more easily negotiable by all people.

Peter L. Lassen

Director, Compliance Division
Architectural and Transportation
Barrier Compliance Board
Washington, D.C.

Contents

The Disabled: Their Needs

Preface

The purpose of this book is to promote an awareness and understanding of the architectural requirements of physically disabled people. State and federal regulations say that buildings must be accessible to and usable by the physically handicapped. As yet, no set of codes is comprehensive enough to satisfy all the needs of the disabled population. Moreover, the regulations and codes vary from state to state and the reasons for the different standards are often not explained. We shall try to explain the reasoning behind recommendations so that architects and planners can use their best judgment in early programming and design decisions.

The book is a result of a search through the literature, interviews with many disabled people, and trips to rehabilitation centers in an effort to find answers for the majority of the physically disabled who can be independent. Sometimes the recommendations from different sources conflict; when there is not agreement on the best way to solve a problem, we either explain the problem to help planners and designers choose a way or use our best judgment in making a recommendation.

We offer some solutions that will help most of the physically disabled by showing how architectural barriers can be eliminated and what suitable aids can be provided in buildings. Even some people who are severely physically disabled can accept employment and lead full lives if they are not prevented from doing so because of difficult access to buildings, architectural barriers within buildings, or lack of appropriate facilities.

This book is primarily concerned with designing spaces and aids for the physically disabled in buildings used by the public, such as educational institutions, public libraries, office buildings, government buildings, airports and other terminals, and apartment buildings. The book is intended for architects, builders, administrators, developers, and others concerned with planning buildings and public spaces. We have not tried to recommend special details for institutions such as hospitals, rehabilitation centers, or nursing homes or to find answers for particular individual problems. We have found that handicapped people want as few special arrangements as possible, and the book has been written with this in mind.

We focus mainly on the requirements of people in wheelchairs because their needs for space are the most demanding. Photographs and drawings are included to illustrate general problems and solutions. Significant dimensions are shown in the illustrations and are therefore omitted from the text except when it is clearer to include them. The human figure shown represents a person 5′6″/1.68 m tall—the fiftieth percentile of U.S. adults is said to be that size. Obviously, if a 5′6″/1.68 m person can reach a certain shelf height, so can a taller person. The transparent template of the wheelchair figure is intended as a useful aid in planning buildings. The figure may be laid over an architectural plan or elevation drawing to illustrate the space requirement of a person in a wheelchair. At the end of the book are tables that summarize standards and recommendations from several sources, with our own recommendations in the last column.

We would like to thank the many people who have helped us with this guide. Some of them are disabled, others are in the field of rehabilitation, and some are both. All of them have encouraged us and expressed the need for a guide of this sort.

We are particularly indebted to the following people:

Robert Amendola
Instructor, Videation and
Spatial Orientation
Carroll Center for the Blind

Beata Anderson
Wheelchair Olympic Champion

Elmer Bartels
Massachusetts Association of Paraplegics

Mary Downing, RPT
Supervising Physical Therapist
Lemuel Shattuck Hospital

Carl V. Granger, MD
Chief of Physical Medicine
and Rehabilitation
Tufts-New England Medical Center

Dorothy Jeffrey
President, Humanities, Inc.

Peter L. Lassen
Director, Compliance Division
Architectural and Transportation
Barrier Compliance Board

Robert Lynch
Architect, AIA

Salvatore Mazzotta
Manager of Data Processing
LeMessurier Associates/SCI

Betsy Pillsbury, Student

Winona Roundtree, Teacher

Edwin Schneider
Professor of Vocational Education
and Technology
University of Vermont

Benjamin F. Smith
Director, Perkins School for the Blind

Harold Stone
Chief of Educational Therapy
Rehabilitation Medicine Service
West Roxbury Veterans Administration

Wesley G. Wall, Jr., MD
Chief of Physical Medicine
and Rehabilitation
Lemuel Shattuck Hospital

". . . it shall be national policy to recognize the inherent right of all citizens, regardless of their physical disability, to the full development of their economic, social, and personal potential, through the free use of the manmade environment." AIA, Conference on a Barrier-Free Environment, January 1974.

This statement has been endorsed by the National Easter Seal Society for Crippled Children and Adults, the President's Committee for Employment of the Handicapped, and the Paralyzed Veterans of America.

But architectural planning that will permit "free use of the manmade environment" is not easy. The requirements of disabled people differ and what may help one person may sometimes hinder another. No arrangement will be perfect for people of every size and with every kind of disability. Therefore, there is a limit to what legislation can do. However, an understanding of the needs of the disabled should open buildings to many more people than it was possible to do in the past.

For this book the disabled are defined as people with sensory, manipulatory, or locomotor disabilities, or a combination of these. The sensory disabled are the blind, the deaf, and those with partial impairment of sight or hearing. The manipulatory disabled are people who have difficulty using one or both hands or arms. The locomotor disabled are those with disabilities that affect mobility—the ambulant and the chairbound disabled. Disabilities of the elderly are also included as they often fit into one or more of these categories. We consider the disabled to be restricted or inconvenienced in their use of buildings if there are "barriers" that restrict people's free passage or if no suitable facilities have been provided to help them.

Because the sensory disabled generally have needs that are different from those of other disabled people, the sections on the blind and the deaf describe the special aids that can be planned and installed in buildings to help them. These special provisions do not conflict with the requirements of the manipulatory and the locomotor disabled and often help to make facilities in public buildings more accessible and easy to use in general.

Although there are, in some cases, conflicting needs among people with different kinds of locomotor disabilities, the recommendations in the section on the chairbound disabled will usually aid the manipulatory and the ambulant disabled as well. To avoid repetition, the sections on the manipulatory and the ambulant disabled deal specifically with problems and recommendations unique to them.

The
Blind

Modern rehabilitation methods, especially training in the use of a long cane, are enabling the blind to go almost anywhere. Guide dogs are suitable for only a small percentage of the blind population. Most blind people are guided through a building on their first visit and thereafter follow a memorized route. The main obstacles for the blind in buildings are unexpected hazards: people moving across their path; movable objects, such as toys and bicycles; open places in the floor; or temporary objects (such as scaffolding or exhibits), rather than permanent fixtures which can be memorized. In any case, unnecessary projections and sudden variations in level should be avoided. Outdoors, benches and other street furniture should not obstruct passage on public walks.

A building designed specifically for the blind—with narrow corridors and no large open spaces—would be far from ideal for everyone else. However, the following simple aids are helpful to the blind and often to people with other disabilities as well.

Steps and Stairs
Steps and stairs should not have either open risers or square, protruding nosings. This is also helpful for the ambulant disabled.

Acoustics
Sound-reflecting walls are preferred to sound-absorbing walls because the blind use their sense of hearing to guide them. The blind also use sound reflected up from walking surfaces to orient themselves. Carpeting, which absorbs or muffles sound, is not desirable in a building that is to be used by the blind. Note, however, that a "live" acoustical environment makes hearing more difficult for the partly deaf and that many of the ambulant disabled prefer a nonskid, carpeted floor. The acoustical design of a space should therefore be determined by the needs of the majority of people who will use it.

Walking Surfaces
Changes of material in walking surfaces can be used to indicate the proximity of entrances, restrooms, steps and stairs, or potentially hazardous areas. Note, however, that some floor materials affect the mobility of the ambulant and the chairbound disabled.

Hardware
Doors that lead to dangerous areas, such as boiler rooms, loading platforms, and equipment rooms, should be identified by operating hardware that is knurled or roughened.

Signals and Signs
Ideally, all information throughout a building should be communicated both audibly and visibly. Signals, such as fire alarms, can easily be supplemented with audible warnings or directions. Elevators can be equipped with single and double audible impulse signals to indicate the direction of travel. If possible, signs and other written or graphic material should be accompanied by recorded messages. Where this is not practical, and the blind must rely on printed information alone, there are three options: braille, large letters and numbers, and raised letters and numbers.

Most totally blind people who can travel independently read and rely on braille. For some, these are the only characters they know as they have never seen or been taught Roman letters or Arabic numbers. However, many legally blind people are partly sighted and can see and read information that is printed in a simple, light, sans serif typeface. The characters should be white, set against a dark background, and at least 3/16″/5 mm high (18 point). Therefore, for signs or other communications involving more than a single letter or number, a combination of braille for the totally blind, and large letters and numbers for the partly sighted, would meet the needs of the majority of the visually handicapped. Raised letters and numbers are not recommended for messages of more than a single character because it is very difficult to "read" a quantity of raised type by touch.

However, where only single letters and numbers are required, as for elevator buttons and apartment or room numbers, raised letters and numbers are recommended because they can be easily deciphered and understood by the majority of the visually handicapped. The only people who might have trouble with raised letters and numbers are the totally blind who have not learned the alphabet or Arabic numbers. For them, braille adjacent to the single characters is recommended. Raised letters and numbers should be set in a simple, light, sans serif typeface, at least .035″/8.9 mm from the wall, and a minimum of ½″/13 mm high (48 point). Only upper case letters should be used as lower case letters are difficult to distinguish by touch. In an elevator, braille and

Tactual map for the blind

raised letters and numbers should be located next to buttons in the cab. Each floor should be identified by braille and raised letters or numbers, applied to the elevator door frame at least 5′0″/1.52 m and no more than 5′6″/1.68 m above the floor, on the right side when exiting.

All signs and single letters and numbers should be set at a standard, consistent height throughout a building—a minimum of 5′0″/1.52 m and a maximum of 5′6″/1.68 m from the floor—so that the blind will know where to find them. Signs, letters, and numbers at doors should be positioned at a standard, consistent distance from the doorjamb—a minimum of 6″/15 cm and a maximum of 18″/46 cm from the jamb.

The Deaf

The Manipulatory Disabled

Few people are totally deaf; many people who are hard of hearing or considered legally deaf can hear with comprehension in an acoustically favorable space without the ambient noise that is typically present in restaurants or lobbies. Certain special aids that will help both the deaf and the partly deaf can easily be included in buildings.

Signals and Signs
Warnings and directions should be equipped with clearly noticeable visual signals, such as flashing lights. Fire alarms, door bells, and telephones should all have visible as well as audible signals.

At least one receiver in a group of telephones should have an amplifier for the hard of hearing; this can be arranged with the telephone company. Private telephones can also be equipped with an amplifier and/or a light signal in addition to the bell.

Public address systems should be clear and audible but not unusually loud.

Signs should be clear and easily noticeable so that people do not have to ask for directions; some deaf people have difficulty talking and being understood.

People with manipulatory disabilities have impaired function in one or both arms or hands. They have difficulties in buildings if there are heavy doors with inconveniently placed or shaped door handles or a lack of automatic controls.

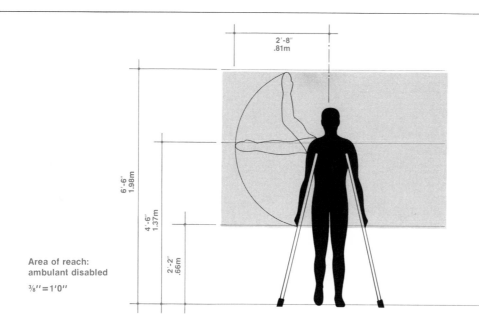

2'-8"
.81m

6'-6"
1.98m

4'-6"
1.37m

2'-2"
.66m

Area of reach:
ambulant disabled

³⁄₈" = 1'0"

The ambulant disabled are people who walk with difficulty and insecurity, using canes, braces, crutches, or other aids. They include many of the elderly, people temporarily disabled, and people with an amputated leg or foot. Because stooping and bending are difficult for them, many of the ambulant disabled have trouble changing easily from standing and sitting positions.

In general, the specifications given for the chairbound (for widths of passages, adequate space in elevators, bathrooms) apply also to the ambulant disabled, although their needs are neither so special nor so restrictive as those of people in wheelchairs. However, certain requirements of the ambulant disabled differ from those of the chairbound.

Area of reach: ambulant
and chairbound disabled

⅜″=1′0″

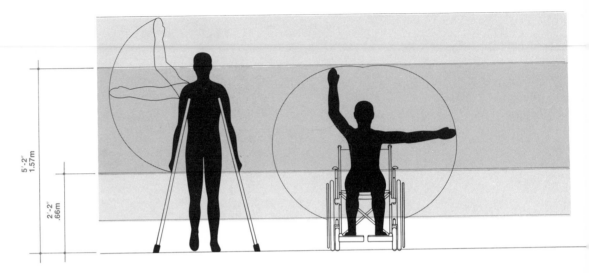

5′-2″
1.57m

2′-2″
.66m

Area of Reach While Standing

Handles, controls, switches, storage elements, and important items such as oven or freezer compartments should be within the reach of a standing person so that stooping is not necessary. The lower range of reach of a standing person is also within the reach of the chairbound.

Ramps and Walks

Many of the ambulant disabled find stairs easier to negotiate than ramps (which are necessary for the chairbound). If ramps are to be used by the ambulant disabled as the main means of entry, a minimum gradient of slope is best, with 1:12 (8.33 percent) as a maximum. Hard, level, non-skid surfaces are essential, and all ramps, steps, stairs, sidewalks, doorways, platforms, and related areas should be kept dry and free of snow and ice.

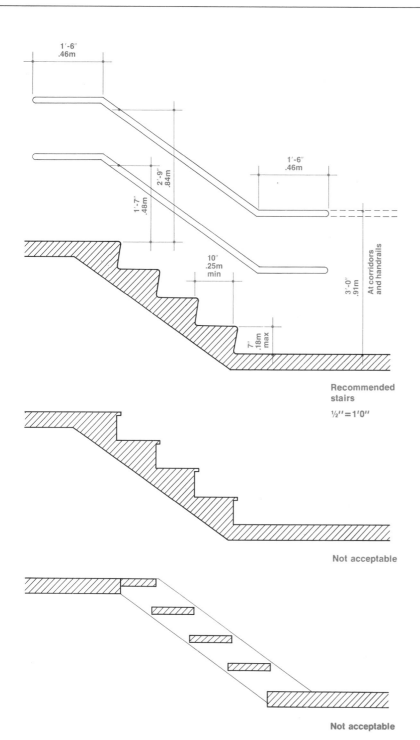

1'-6"
.46m

1'-6"
.46m

2'-9"
.84m

1'-7"
.48m

10"
.25m
min

At corridors
and handrails

3'-0"
.91m

7"
.18m
max

**Recommended
stairs**

½"=1'0"

Not acceptable

Not acceptable

Steps and Stairs

Steps and stairs should have nonprotruding nosings so that people with stiff joints, braces, artificial legs, or other leg or stability problems will not catch their toes as they climb.

Handrails should be oval or round with 1½"/4 cm hand clearance between the rails and the wall: 1½"/4 cm clearance will provide ease of grip but will prevent the hand or wrist from slipping between the handrail and the wall if the person loses balance. Handrails should be positioned on both sides of steps and stairs and should extend beyond the first and last steps on at least one side and preferably on both to allow people with long leg braces to pull themselves beyond these points. To guard against falls and to help children, some codes require another, lower handrail.

Steps, stairs, and handrails should not be made of slippery material.

The
Chairbound
Disabled

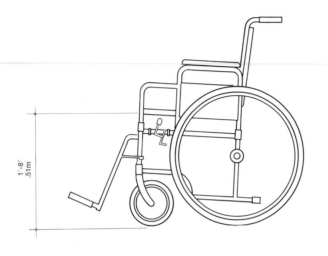

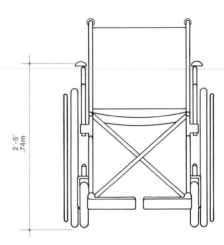

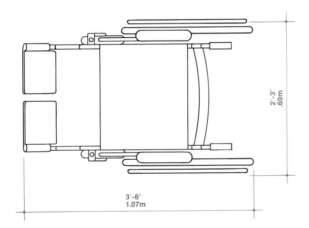

**Wheelchair: adult size
with removable arms**

¾"=1'0"

The chairbound are people who depend upon wheelchairs for mobility. Although some of them are able to stand while transferring to and from a wheelchair, the strictly chairbound are unable to walk or stand with or without assistance.

The chairbound are not the majority of the disabled population, but since their requirements for mobility demand the most space, our recommended dimensions are based on the requirements of the chairbound, except where we specifically recommend another solution for a different disability. The dimensions will also, in most cases, benefit people with other disabilities.

The Wheelchair
The wheelchair used most by independent chairbound people is the collapsible adult size, with rear propelling wheels. It varies, with features such as removable arms and back. Since the wheelchair with removable arms is very common and indeed nec-

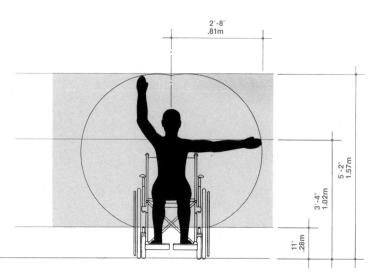

2'-8"
.81m

5'-2"
1.57m

3'-4"
1.02m

11"
.28m

Area of reach:
chairbound disabled

⅜"=1'0"

essary for many of the chairbound, the width of this type of wheelchair should be used as the standard when planning spaces. Although one would wish for improvements, such as lighter weight and greater durability, this type of wheelchair at present offers the best compromise for independent chairbound people.

Wheelchair Transfer Space
In determining space for wheelchairs it is important to understand the motions necessary to make a transfer into or out of a wheelchair.

Wheelchair transfer to or from a car seat, toilet seat, shower seat, bed, or other furniture is accomplished in one of three basic ways: via the front, rear, or side of the wheelchair. The front transfer usually requires a twist turn with the aid of supports, such as grab bars. A removable or zipper back to the wheelchair makes a rear transfer possible, but this type of transfer is less common. A severely disabled person usu-

ally has a wheelchair with removable arms, making a side transfer possible. Since the side transfer is the only transfer some people can accomplish, space for the wheelchair beside a seat or bed is desirable. Ideally, there should be space on both sides of a seat or bed to allow people a choice of directions because some people, such as victims of stroke or arthritis, can only transfer from one side. This also allows room for another person to support a severely disabled person.

Area of Reach
The upper area of reach of a chairbound person is within the low to middle range of a standing person's. Therefore, necessary elements, such as control buttons and mechanisms, countertops, and important shelves, should be located within this common range.

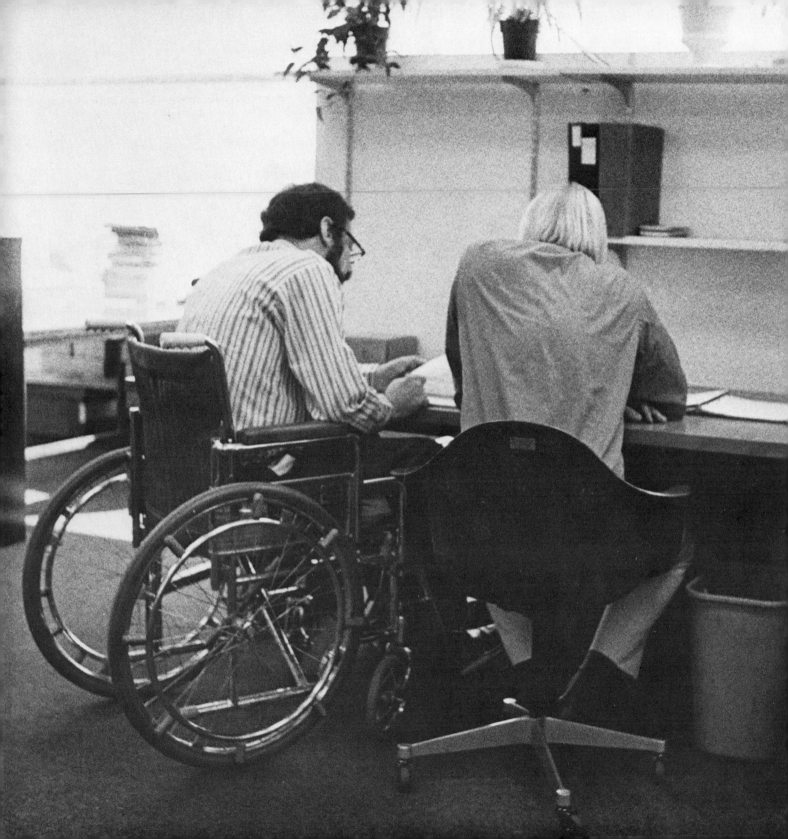

Site
Development

Symbol of Access
The international wheelchair symbol of access should be used to mark appropriate parking spaces, entrances, ramps, and accessible travel routes. Inside a building, the symbol should be used to designate elevators, restrooms, and public telephones that can be used by the chairbound disabled.

Transportation
Since most cities do not yet provide public transportation that is usable by the chairbound, they have to rely mainly on taxis and on private cars that can be equipped with the necessary hand controls, brakes, and driving aids. To allow complete independence for the disabled, the folded wheelchair can be stowed in the car and removed upon arrival at the destination.

Sequence: transfer from
wheelchair into car

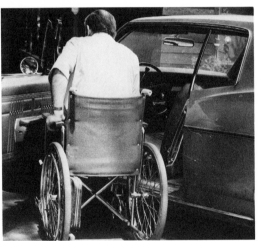

1

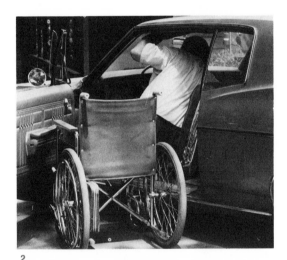

2

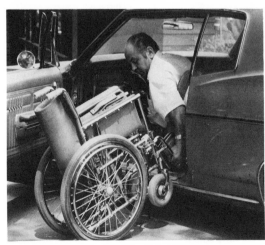

3

Parking spaces for the disabled

⅛″=1′0″

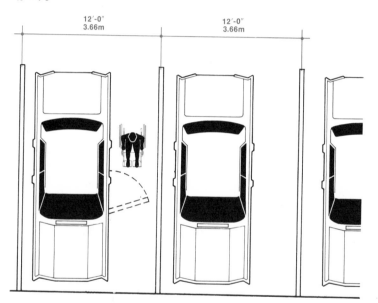

12′-0″
3.66m

12′-0″
3.66m

Parking

It is important to provide a level parking surface near public buildings so that people can transfer easily and safely between their cars and their wheelchairs. Parking stalls for the disabled should be located as close as possible to the main entrance of the building and the approach from parking to the entrance should be either level or ramped. To allow the disabled person to fully open the car door and place the wheelchair next to the car for transfer, the parking stalls should be extra wide. When the wheelchair is positioned next to the car, the wheelchair should be level with the car, not on a higher or lower grade. Passages within the parking area, or that lead to and from the parking area, should be planned for good visibility. They should not lead behind moving vehicles since the low height of people in wheelchairs makes them hard to see, especially for a driver using a rearview mirror.

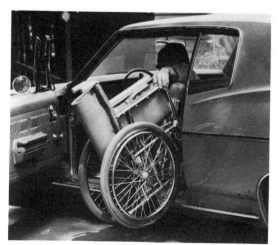

4

5

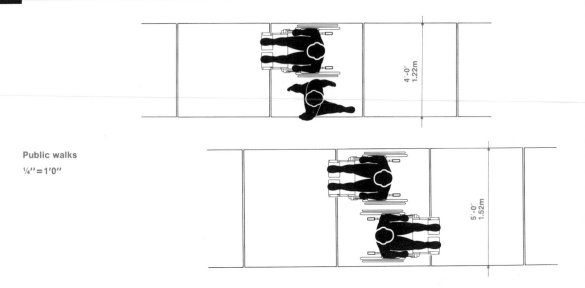

Public walks

¼″=1′0″

Public Walks

To ensure easy wheelchair passage, public walks should be kept open. They should not be obstructed by street furniture, such as benches, or by any other objects (see The Blind). Since the wheels of a wheelchair are not very wide, usually about 1″/25.4 mm, there should be no gratings or other openings along the surface of the walk. In areas where walks can be obstructed by snow or made slippery by ice and rain, it is important to protect the walks so that the chairbound can use them safely. Covered walks enable the chairbound to approach and enter a building without assistance in all kinds of weather.

In different codes, the width of public walks is given as either 4′0″/1.22 m or 5′0″/1.52 m. A width of 4′0″/1.22 m permits one pedestrian and one person in a wheelchair to pass each other. It also allows a wheelchair to make a 90-degree turn in the path without backing up. We suggest a width of 5′0″/1.52 m, more than twice the maximum width of a wheelchair, to allow two wheelchairs to pass each other and one wheelchair to make a tight 180-degree turn without having to reverse when making the turn.

The approach to at least one entrance of a building (preferably the main entrance) should be level or ramped. Gradients on public walks without ramps should not exceed 1:20 (5 percent); if handrails are provided, a gradient of 1:12 (8.33 percent) is acceptable. The best condition is a continuous surface with no steps and with no abrupt changes in level greater than ½″/13 mm.

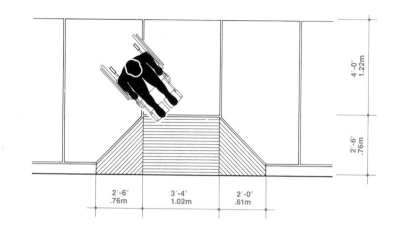

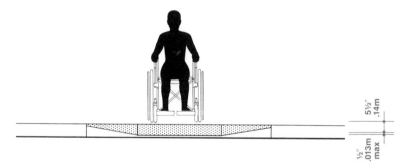

Curb cut: 1:12 (8.33%)
recommended slope

1:6 (16.66%) maximum
slope

¼"=1'0"

Curb Cuts

Curb cuts should, wherever possible, be
sloped at a gradient of 1:12 (8.33 percent)
to allow a wheelchair to make a grade
change gradually. If the slope is too steep,
the wheelchair may tip over backwards as
it goes up, or the footrests may catch as it
goes down. If a slope of 1:12 is impractical
(because the curb cut then becomes too
long for a narrow walk), a gradient of up to
1:6 (16.66 percent) is acceptable.

The edges of the curb cut should be sloped
rather than cut sharply or protected by a
planting strip so that pedestrians (especially the blind) will not trip over an edge
and fall.

The curb cut should meet the street as
smoothly as possible. If a lip is unavoid-
able where the slope and the street meet, it
should be no more than ½"/13 mm high.

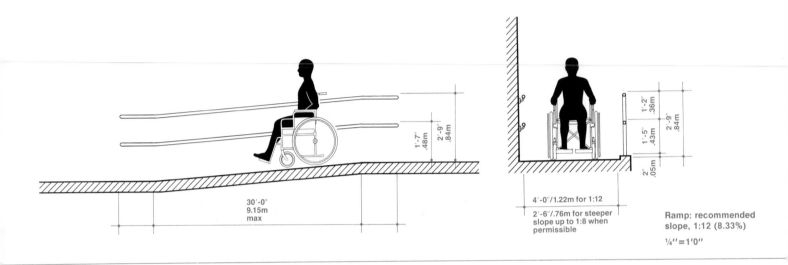

1'-7"
.48m

2'-9"
.84m

1'-2"
.36m

1'-5"
.43m

2'-9"
.84m

2"
.05m

30'-0"
9.15m
max

4'-0"/1.22m for 1:12

2'-6"/.76m for steeper
slope up to 1:8 when
permissible

Ramp: recommended
slope, 1:12 (8.33%)

¼" = 1'0"

Ramps

A wheelchair weighs from 31 to 68 pounds, and it is extremely tiring for most of the chairbound to propel themselves up a ramp, especially if it is at the maximum slope of 1:12 (8.33 percent). For the descent on a long or steep ramp there is the danger of loss of control. Because the wheelchair is slowed by the hands and not by a brake, an attempt to control its downward speed could cause friction burns on the hands. Level rest platforms are therefore necessary at 30'0"/9.15 m intervals for ascent and descent on a long ramp. Level platforms are also necessary wherever a ramp changes direction as it is very difficult to turn a wheelchair on a slope.

At entries, a ramp should be provided if there is a change of level. A ramp leading to or away from a doorway should include a level platform that extends beyond the width of the doorway on both sides to allow the wheelchair to be positioned while the door is being opened or closed (see Doors and Doorways).

Because handrails are used by some chairbound people to pull themselves up a ramp, an additional lower round or oval continuous handrail should be provided on each side, extending beyond the slope at the top and bottom of a ramp.

Ramps should have curbs on both sides so that a wheelchair cannot accidentally run off the ramp. Curbs can also help to brake a wheelchair in an emergency.

There should be at least 5'0"/1.52 m of straight clearance at the bottom of a ramp.

Nonskid surfaces are essential. If possible, ramps should be protected from the elements. In any case, they should be kept free of ice and snow.

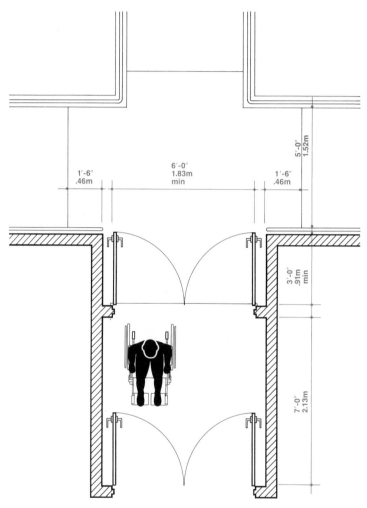

1'-6"
.46m

6'-0"
1.83m
min

1'-6"
.46m

5'-0"
1.52m

3'-0"
.91m
min

7'-0"
2.13m

Entrance vestibule with ramps

¼"=1'0"

Entry
The disabled should be able to enter a building through primary entrances and not service areas. Buildings should not have revolving doors or turnstiles as the sole means of entry since they are not passable by the chairbound and are hazardous to the ambulant disabled and the blind. All entrances that also serve as emergency exits should be accessible to and usable by the chairbound. In a multistory building, at least one accessible entrance should lead to an elevator.

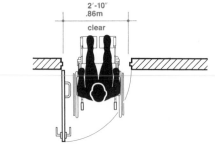

2'-10"
.86m
clear

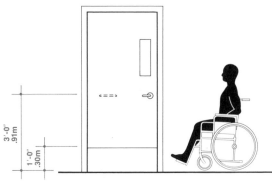

3'-0"
.91m

1'-0"
.30m

**Side-hinged
swinging door**

¼"=1'0"

Doors and Doorways

Doorways should be wide enough to allow
easy passage for a wheelchair. Some codes
specify a 34"/86 cm clear opening width
for doorways. Although this is more than is
needed for the wheelchair to pass through
the opening, less space requires greater
precision in the wheelchair operation and
restricts the space needed by the person's
arms and hands in turning the wheels. The
wheelchair needs more room if turns have
to be made.

Each leaf of a double-leaf door should be
wide enough so that only one door needs
to be open to allow passage of a wheelchair.

A level space or platform at least 5'0"/
1.52 m wide should extend a minimum of
1'0"/0.30 m on either side of a doorway
to allow the disabled to maneuver the
wheelchair while opening or closing the
door. The best arrangement is a level
platform that extends 1'6"/0.46 m on the
side toward which the door opens.

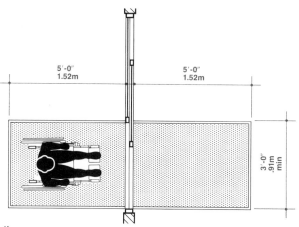

5'-0"
1.52m

5'-0"
1.52m

3'-0"
.91m
min

**Automatic
sliding door**

¼"=1'0"

If two doors are close together, as in an entrance foyer, there should be space between them for the 48″/122 cm length required by the wheelchair, including the person's feet extending beyond the footrests. There should also be space for maneuvering so that the first door can swing shut without catching the wheelchair.

The manual push or pull on a door should not exceed 8 pounds/3.63 kg since more than that requires setting the brake on the wheelchair. However, on a main entrance door, 8 pounds/3.63 kg push or pull might be insufficient to hold the door against wind pressure. Therefore, at entrances, we recommend doors that cannot be blown open, such as automatic doors or doors with time delay closers. We also recommend automatic garage doors. Inside a building, sliding or folding doors are preferred; however, side-hinged doors are satisfactory if they have an additional pull-handle on the hinged side of the door. This permits the chairbound to close the door without being forced to position the wheelchair in the path of the door's swing when reaching for the door handle.

Door handles should be either lever-type or oval in shape and easy to grip to help people with manipulatory disabilities who might have difficulty gripping round doorknobs.

We recommend a viewing panel in a door, especially in double-action swinging doors. The panel should be placed low enough to give people in wheelchairs good visibility and to allow them to be seen.

A kickplate at the bottom of a door protects the door from the impact of a wheelchair's footrest. Doors should be specified that have no protruding parts near the area of the footrests, such as the stiles on glass doors, so that they do not catch on a footrest when the chairbound use it to push open the door.

Thresholds are obvious hindrances; if used, they should be feathered on both sides.

Corridors, Passageways, and Floors

Corridors and passageways should be wide enough for a wheelchair to make a 180-degree turn in a continuous movement.

For changes of level, there should be a ramp or a lifting device, such as an inclinator.

Floors should have flat, nonskid surfaces. Carpets should be well fitted to the floor; they should be inset to lie flush with adjacent surfaces. Carpets with deep piles or padding should be avoided as they make passage difficult for both the chairbound and the ambulant disabled.

Elevators

Elevators should be provided in all public buildings of two or more levels since the chairbound disabled can use them independently, whereas they cannot manage escalators and stairs without assistance. At least one elevator should be large enough for a wheelchair and should have access to the main lobby and entrance, main circulation corridor, and other public areas.

Elevator controls and safety devices should be low enough to be within the diagonal reach of a person in a wheelchair. These may be either on the front or the side wall of the elevator. As mentioned, braille symbols and single raised letters and numbers should be located next to standard buttons in the elevator cab and at each floor on the elevator door frame (see The Blind).

Some chairbound people enter into and exit from elevators with large (usually rear) wheels first to avoid the possibility of catching the small wheels in the gap between the floor and the elevator cab. The gap should not be more than ⅜″ / 1 cm.

Automatic leveling should be required so that there is no difference between the levels of the floor and the elevator cab.

The interior dimensions of the elevator cab should allow a wheelchair to enter, turn 180 degrees, and exit easily.

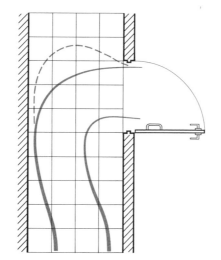

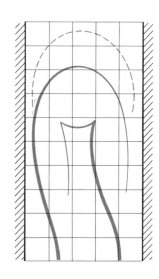

Wheelchair space for turning; dotted line represents line of footrest travel

¼″=1′0″

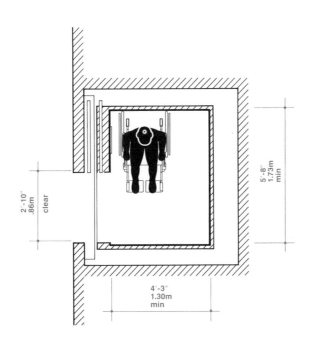

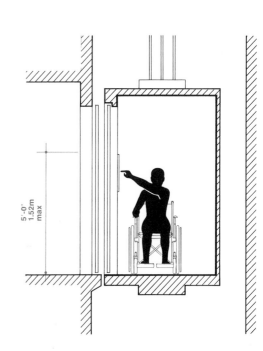

2′-10″ .86m clear

5′-8″ 1.73m min

4′-3″ 1.30m min

5′-0″ 1.52m max

Elevator

¼″=1′0″

Plan

Section

Building Controls

It is important that the chairbound be able to reach controls throughout a building without having to ask for help. One of the principal differences between the requirements of the chairbound and the ambulant disabled is in the area of reach (see The Chairbound Disabled, Area of Reach). The seated position of the chairbound gives them an area of reach that is lower than that of a standing person. Therefore, the height of important controls, equipment, and storage areas should be in the range common to both the chairbound and the standing ambulant disabled.

Controls, such as light switches, thermostats, electrical outlets, fire alarms, call buttons, air conditioner controls, window hardware, and drapery pulls, should be easy to use and placed no higher than 4'0"/1.22 m above the floor, within the area of reach that is common to both the chairbound and the ambulant disabled.

Shelves and Counters

So that there can be some part of a storage wall suitable for the chairbound, the ambulant disabled, and the ablebodied, all of whom have different minimum and maximum areas of reach, shelves should be full height from floor to ceiling. The usual system of shelves above and below counters does not make use of the space directly above the counter, the most convenient height for disabled people. A full wall of shelves therefore offers some storage within reach for the ambulant and the chairbound disabled.

Where a writing surface is required, as, for example, in a bank or library, at least one 30"/76 cm- to 33"/84 cm-high counter or tabletop should be provided for the chairbound. There should be clearance below the counter or tabletop to give the chairbound knee space under the writing surface so that they can position themselves close to it.

Public Telephones

At least one public telephone in a building should be set low enough to be readily accessible to people in wheelchairs. When a telephone is set low for the chairbound it can be easily used by other people if a folding seat is provided in the booth or enclosure. If booths are provided, they should be 4'0"/1.22 m to 5'0"/1.52 m deep and wide enough to accommodate a wheelchair. A wall-hung telephone with a ceiling- or wall-mounted baffle wall on each side is also satisfactory.

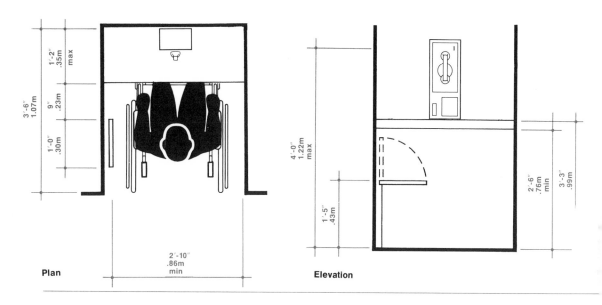

Telephone alcove
½″=1′0″

Plan

2′-10″
.86m
min

3′-6″
1.07m

1′-2″
.35m
max

9″
.23m

1′-0″
.30m

Elevation

4′-0″
1.22m
max

1′-5″
.43m

2′-6″
.76m
min

3′-3″
.99m

Drinking Fountains

To allow knee space under the fountain, we recommend the type of drinking fountain unit that projects out from the wall rather than one that is fully recessed. To avoid creating hazards, especially for the blind, the best location for drinking fountains is in alcoves away from the trafficways. Spouts and hand controls should be installed at the front of all units. It is also useful to have both hand- and foot-operated controls.

Washing Machines and Dryers

At least one washing machine and dryer in each laundry room should be front-loading; the coin slot and controls should also be on the front of the machine. Controls should not be set higher than 4′0″/1.22 m.

Front transfer

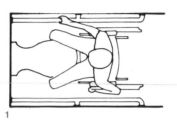

1

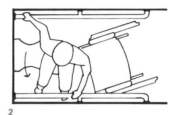

2

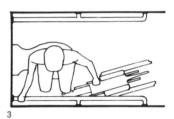

3

Front transfer with twist turn

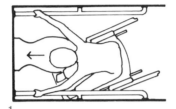

1

2

3

Side transfer with diagonal turn

1

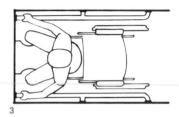

2

3

Restrooms and bathrooms are the most difficult spaces to make convenient and easily usable because the fixtures that would allow the most flexibility of use are not yet readily available on the market. Two items that would facilitate the use of restrooms and bathrooms are swing-away or removable grab bars and adjustable-height toilet seats. Until these are manufactured, compromise solutions must suffice and architects must use their best judgment in planning spaces for people with different disabilities.

Transfer
As described under The Chairbound Disabled, transfer from a wheelchair to a toilet seat is accomplished usually from the side or front of the wheelchair. If adjustable grab bars could be provided, the ideal arrangement would be to have space on both sides of the toilet to allow people a choice of directions from which to transfer. A satisfactory solution is to plan alternate right- and left-side transfer spaces in a row of toilet stalls.

4

Side transfer

1

2

3

Baffle Walls and Partitions

Care should be taken that baffle walls and partitions that block the entrance door from public view do not impede access for a person in a wheelchair. Ceiling- or wall-mounted baffles and partitions, open at the bottom, are preferred to floor mountings because they do not obstruct the footrests on the wheelchair.

Toilet Stalls

At least one toilet stall in each public restroom should be planned and equipped for the disabled. Adequate room should be provided for a wheelchair to turn as it enters the stall. The door of the toilet stall should open outward: otherwise the wheelchair might prevent it from closing. Also, if a disabled person falls, an outward-swinging door can easily be opened, but an inward-swinging door might be obstructed by the person's body.

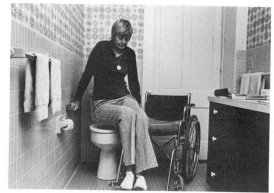

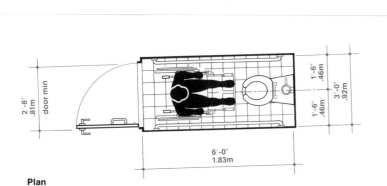

Plan

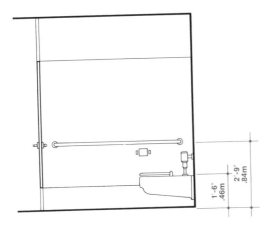

Elevation

**Minimum toilet stall for
the disabled—more
suitable for the ambulant
than the chairbound**

¼″=1′0″

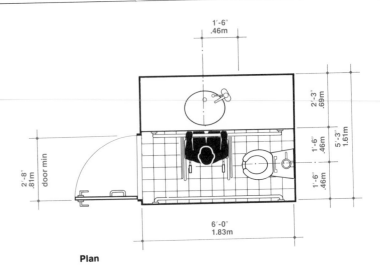

Plan

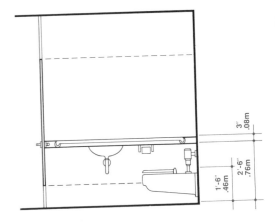

Elevation

**Suggested restroom/
lavatory 1: toilet stall
(or lavatory) with
washbasin; ample space
for turning a wheelchair**

¼″=1′0″

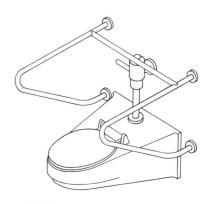

A standard arrangement suitable for the ambulant disabled but not the chairbound

Arrangements

Several arrangements of toilets with grab bars are possible and code requirements differ from state to state. The least expensive and most widely used arrangement provides long grab bars attached to the side walls on either side of a 3'0"/0.91 m-wide toilet stall. This arrangement serves the ambulant disabled very well and is usable by many of the chairbound. However, it requires a transfer from either the front or the rear of the wheelchair.

An often recommended variation of this arrangement provides a set of grab bars attached to and cantilevered from the wall behind the toilet. Again, this arrangement serves the ambulant disabled very well. But we do not recommend it for the chairbound since it requires a front or rear transfer, with the added disadvantage that the grab bars cannot be as long as they could if they were attached to the side walls.

Our suggested Restroom/Lavatory 1 is, we think, a great improvement over the standard 3'0"/10.91 m-wide stall recommended in many codes. It includes a built-in washbasin and counter in the stall or lavatory within reach of the seated position on the toilet. The space under the counter allows knee space so that a wheelchair may be positioned for a diagonal transfer (much easier for most chairbound people than front transfer). The long grab bars are the same as for the standard 3'0"/0.91 m-wide stall. This is an attractive arrangement that both the able-bodied and the disabled could find helpful.

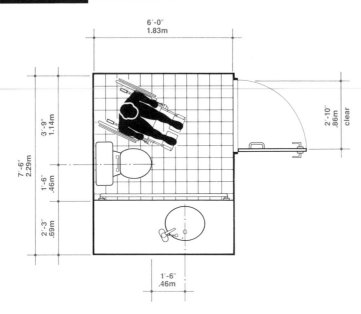

6'-0"
1.83m

7'-6"
2.29m

3'-9"
1.14m

1'-6"
.46m

2'-3"
.69m

2'-10"
.86m
clear

1'-6"
.46m

Suggested restroom/
lavatory 2

¼"=1'0"

The Suggested Restroom/Lavatory 2 also includes a built-in washbasin within reach of the toilet, with knee space under the counter. The greater width of the stall allows room for a one side transfer from a wheelchair positioned beside the toilet. This arrangement can be used by many of the chairbound, although the ambulant disabled and the elderly might prefer to have bars on both sides of the toilet.

The most convenient arrangement for both the ambulant and the chairbound disabled would be to provide space on both sides of the toilet with hinged, swing-away, or removable grab bars. It would then be possible to adjust the grab bars to suit the individual. Unfortunately, adjustable grab bars are not readily available and would have to be specially designed and manufactured.

The architect and owner must decide which of the various arrangements is most suitable for the particular situation. On the ground floor of a multilevel building, it might be advisable to provide toilet stalls that are most suitable for the chairbound. These would be big enough to include space beside the toilet for the wheelchair (allowing transfer from alternate sides in more than one stall) and a washbasin within reach of the seated position on the toilet. Narrower stalls with grab bars on both sides of the toilet could then be provided on the upper floors for the ambulant disabled. This arrangement allows a greater number of stalls suitable for the ambulant disabled, who are in fact the majority of the disabled population.

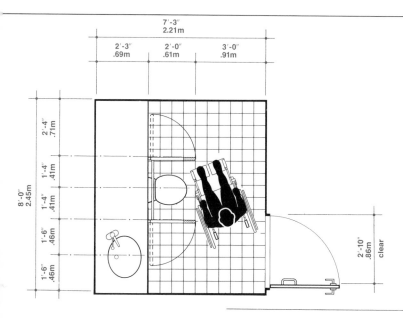

7'-3"
2.21m

2'-3"
.69m

2'-0"
.61m

3'-0"
.91m

2'-4"
.71m

1'-4"
.41m

1'-4"
.41m

1'-6"
.46m

1'-6"
.46m

8'-0"
2.45m

2'-10"
.86m clear

Suggested restroom/
lavatory 3

¼"=1'0"

Toilets

The toilet should be either wall-hung or with a narrow understructure that recedes abruptly, to allow close positioning of a wheelchair without the footrest hitting the toilet bowl. The flush control should be within easy reach, not too close behind the seated person.

Regulations call for various toilet seat heights, with 18"/46 cm, 19"/48 cm, and 20"/51 cm the most commonly given. This is higher than the standard 16"/41 cm toilet seat height so that the seats of the wheelchair and the toilet will be at about the same height. The 20"/51 cm height lines up best with the seat height of the wheelchair but is too high for the average person's feet to reach the floor for balance. Therefore, paraplegics with strong arms might prefer the standard height of 16"/41 cm while some quadriplegics and the am-

bulant disabled, who have difficulty in lowering themselves (especially those with severe arthritis), might prefer the greater height of 20"/51 cm. We recommend a compromise height of 18"/46 cm, which is also usable by the ablebodied. There is a definite need for a toilet to be manufactured with a variable height seat that can be easily adjusted by different users.

A seat extender can be used on a standard toilet to raise the height of the seat. In a public restroom or private bathroom, the extender could be permanently attached. One advantage of the extender is that clear space is provided between the seat and the extender which some people need to reach themselves for personal hygiene. One objection is that they are sometimes unstable.

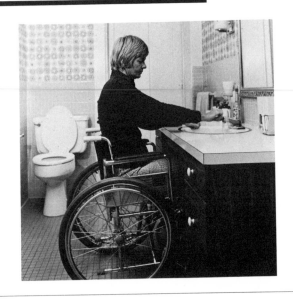

Washbasin for the
disabled

Grab Bars and Hardware

Grab bars at the toilet, tub, and shower are
particularly important for balance, stability, and safety. Different positions are for
different functions: horizontal grab bars
are used for pushing up; vertical grab bars
for pulling up. Although angled grab bars
can be used for both pushing and pulling
up, they do not serve either function as
well as horizontal or vertical grab bars because they require a stronger grip. All grab
bars should be 1½″/4 cm in diameter, installed with 1½″/4 cm clearance between
the bar and the wall. This gives people a
good grip and yet the 1½″/4 cm space is
not wide enough to allow the arm to slip
through, which would be hazardous. In an
apartment or housing development, block-
ing should be built into the bathroom walls
so that grab bars can be installed later to
suit each tenant. In the bathroom of a private house, the installation of grab bars
can, of course, be specially planned to suit
the needs of the disabled person.

Washbasins

Washbasins should preferably be 27″/69
cm deep with a narrow apron to allow
knee room underneath. The hot water and
drain pipes should be insulated to safe-
guard a person in a wheelchair who has no
sensory perception in the legs. Maximum
water temperatures should not exceed 120
degrees F/49 degrees C. Faucets should
have safety mixing valves and should be the
single-level type for people whose hands
are weak.

It is helpful to have the lever controls located to one side of the washbasin.

If possible, a public restroom should include a washbasin positioned within reach
from the toilet for the chairbound disabled.

1. **Space for a wheelchair beside the toilet**

2. **Toilet with recessed base**

3. **Long grab bar beside toilet**

4. **27"/69cm-deep counter**

5. **Toilet paper within reach at the side of the toilet**

6. **Washbasin within reach of the seated position on the toilet**

7. **Mixing faucet, lever handle, within reach of the seated position on the toilet**

8. **Knee space under counter, drain pipe covered or insulated**

9. **Mirror, lower edge no higher than 36"/91cm**

10. **Outswinging bathroom door, lever handle**

11. **Door pull, hinge side of door**

Accessories

Towel dispensers, soap holders, and other accessories should be within reach of both the ambulant and the chairbound disabled. They should be positioned no more than 40"/102 cm above the floor. Mirrors should be low enough for people seated in wheelchairs to see themselves. We recommend a full-length mirror in each restroom or bathroom.

All protruding hardware and fixtures, such as paper holders, soap dishes, towel bars, and bathtub fixtures, should be strong and mounted firmly enough to support at least 250 pounds/113.50 kg (deadweight) for 5 minutes without permanent deflection, as a disabled person is apt to use anything available for support.

Suggested restroom/lavatory 2

Private bathroom suitable for most of the disabled

1. Space for a wheelchair beside the toilet

2. Toilet with recessed base

3. Long grab bar beside toilet

4. 27"/69 cm-deep counter

5. Toilet paper within reach at the side of the toilet

6. Washbasin within reach of the seated position on the toilet

7. Mixing faucet, lever handle, within reach of the seated position on the toilet

8. Knee space under counter, drain pipe covered or insulated

9. Mirror, lower edge no higher than 36"/91 cm

10. Outswinging bathroom door, lever handle

11. Door pull, hinge side of door

12. Medicine cabinet on side wall within reach

13. Platform at end of tub

14. Grab bar, end and back side of tub

15. Small shower stall

Arrangements

The specifications for public restrooms also apply to lavatories, half bathrooms, and private bathrooms. There should be space for the wheelchair beside the bathtub or the entrance to the shower, as well as beside the toilet. In a private house, particular bathroom arrangements can be made to suit the individual. In an apartment house or a housing development, space for a wheelchair should be provided on at least one side of the toilet. Since some people can transfer to the toilet from only one side, flexibility would be assured if the bathroom plans could be reversed in alternate apartments or housing units. The best solution is to provide space on both sides of the toilet, with grab bars installed to suit the individual. (The Fokus Society in Sweden recommends including two toilet drains in a bathroom in all plans to allow for a choice in the positioning of the toilet.)

Bathrooms should provide adequate dressing space. A bathroom with shower directly off of the chairbound disabled person's bedroom is most convenient.

Bathtubs and Showers

In many existing bathrooms, the most convenient way to take a bath is from a movable seat, which has two legs outside the bathtub. Transfer from the wheelchair to the bathtub seat is made from the side of the wheelchair, with the arm of the wheelchair removed. The person's legs have to be lifted over the rim of the bathtub. Disabled people can also take a shower in the seated position, and some can lower themselves from the seat into the bathtub.

The bathtub/shower with a platform located at the head (opposite the drain outlet) of the bathtub is the most versatile arrangement for both ablebodied and disabled people because it enables a person to take a shower in either the standing or sitting position.

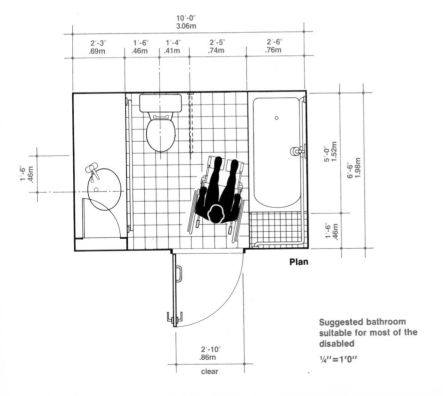

Plan

**Suggested bathroom
suitable for most of the
disabled**

¼″=1′0″

10′-0″
3.06m

2′-3″
.69m

1′-6″
.46m

1′-4″
.41m

2′-5″
.74m

2′-6″
.76m

1′-6″
.46m

5′-0″
1.52m

6′-6″
1.98m

1′-6″
.46m

2′-10″
.86m

clear

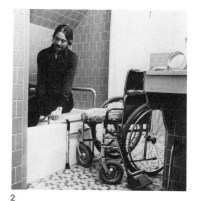

1

2

3

**Transfer from the
wheelchair to a bathtub
seat**

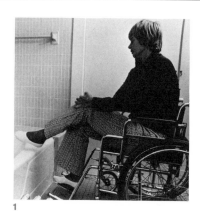
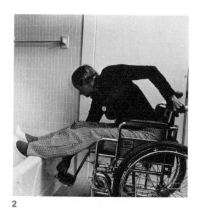
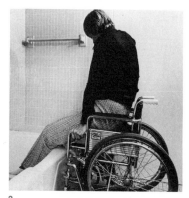

1

2

3

4

5

**Transfer from wheelchair
to built-in bathtub seat**

Bathroom for the disabled

1. Space for a wheelchair
either side of toilet

2. Toilet with recessed base

3. Adjustable height toilet
seat or seat extender

4. Swing-away grab bars

5. 27"/69 cm-deep counter

6. Washbasin within reach of
the seated position on the
toilet

7. Mixing faucet, lever
handle, within reach of
the seated position on the
toilet

8. Knee space under counter,
drain pipe covered or
insulated

9. Mirror, lower edge no
higher than 36"/91 cm

10. Medicine cabinet within
reach

11. Space for transfer to a
shower seat

12. Freestanding shower seat,
can be placed either end of
shower, or removed

13. No curb for shower stall;
the chairbound can wheel
directly into the shower;
shower stall floor slope
to center drain

14. Grab bar, three sides
of shower stall

15. Controls centered on
back wall of shower stall

16. Hand shower

17. Outswinging bathroom
door, lever handle

18. Door pull, hinge side
of door

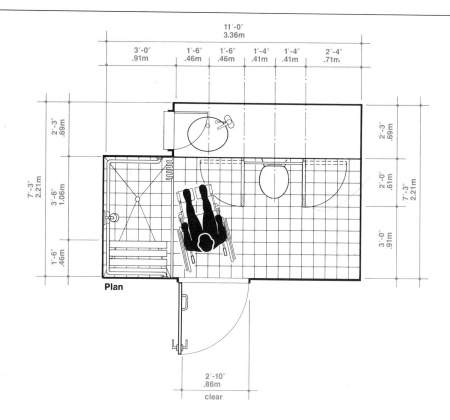

Plan

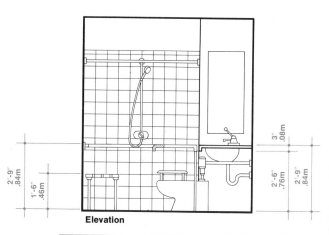

Elevation

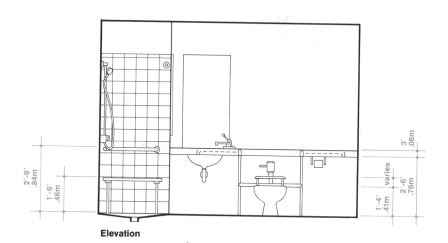

Elevation

Bathroom for the disabled
¼″=1′0″

The easiest way for a disabled person with assistance to take a shower is in a shower chair that can be wheeled directly into a curbless shower stall. However, a conventional stall equipped with a freestanding or permanently installed seat is convenient for most disabled people. The seat can be designed to fold up against the wall when the shower is used by people who are not disabled. Transfer to the shower stall seat from a wheelchair is made in the same way as to the bathtub, from the side of the wheelchair with its arm removed.

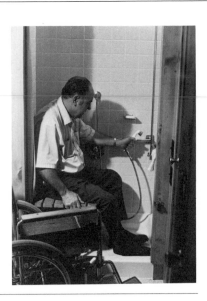

Small
shower stall

Accessories
In a small shower stall, where the stall opening is no wider than 3'0"/0.91 m, a hinged safety bar can be installed at the opening which can be used to maintain balance and to prevent the disabled person from falling out. Horizontal grab bars should be provided on the wall of the stall opposite the seat and on the side wall adjacent to the seat.

In a large shower stall, horizontal grab bars should be installed on all walls.

For either a bathtub/shower or a shower stall, we recommend a hand shower with a flexible hose, located midway on the side wall, with a vertical height adjustment bar. The bar must be as strong as the horizontal grab bars.

The water controls should be located on the side wall, within easy reach from the seated position. The soap holder and the flexible hose hand shower should be on the long wall of the bathtub alcove or shower stall, as shown in Suggested Plans.

Drain plug operators should be lever-type.

It is difficult to design a kitchen that is suitable for the ablebodied, the ambulant disabled, and the chairbound, as there is so much variation in their areas of reach. Kitchen design, however, is not so crucial as bathroom design; a typical kitchen, provided it has adequate turnaround room, while never perfect, does not present the total spatial barrier to the disabled that the typical bathroom does.

Floor Space

For the chairbound, there should be enough floor space so that a wheelchair can move around easily. Although the ambulant disabled might prefer a galley kitchen where counters on both sides can be used for support, they can also manage in an open kitchen. It is most essential that people in wheelchairs have unobstructed wheeling space around the refrigerator, stove, sink, storage areas, and table.

Counter Heights

Although a counter height of 30"/76 cm to 33"/84 cm, with undercounter clearance, is preferred by most people in wheelchairs, it might be awkwardly low for other people using the kitchen. The standard 36"/91 cm counter height is acceptable if a working space or pullout shelf is also provided at a height of 30"/76 cm.

Sinks

A shallow sink with the drain at the rear and with clearance below enables a person in a wheelchair to face the sink and be close to it. For the ambulant disabled and the elderly it is helpful to have room for a chair or stool at the sink. As in bathrooms, the hot water and drain pipes must be insulated so that people without sensory perception in the legs will not be hurt if their legs touch the pipes.

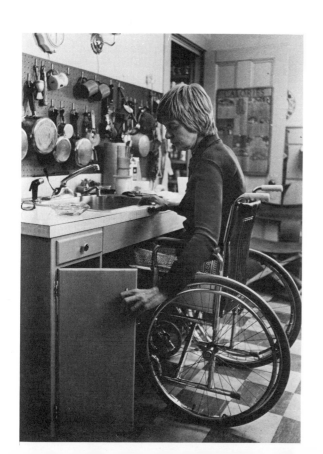

Seating space at kitchen sink

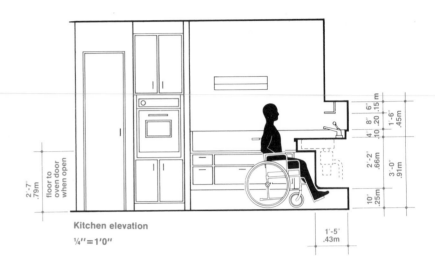

Kitchen elevation

¼″=1′0″

Refrigerators

A two-door, side-by-side refrigerator-freezer is best for both the chairbound and the ambulant disabled because it allows for variation in areas of reach. However, if the standard one-door refrigerator is provided, the freezing compartment should be at the bottom for the chairbound or at the top for the ambulant disabled. The self-defrosting models are, of course, most convenient.

Built-in oven at counter level

Ovens

A built-in oven at counter level is best for the ambulant disabled, the chairbound, and the elderly. An oven in the lower part of a stove is hazardous for the chairbound because they can burn their legs on the hot door without realizing it. It is also a difficult height for the ambulant disabled and the elderly to reach easily.

An oven door at counter height allows the chairbound to position themselves close enough to lift food from the pullout rack to the oven door and then to a counter. The oven door, hinged at the bottom, protects the legs from splatters and spills.

Cooktops

The cooktop controls should be at the front; reaching over a hot burner or pot is hazardous for everyone and particularly for the chairbound, who have a lower range of reach. A cooktop height of 30″/76

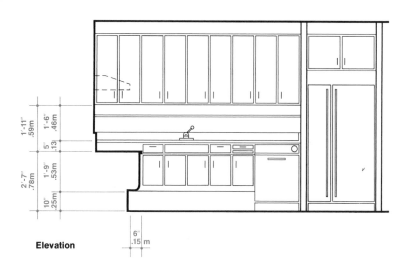

Elevation

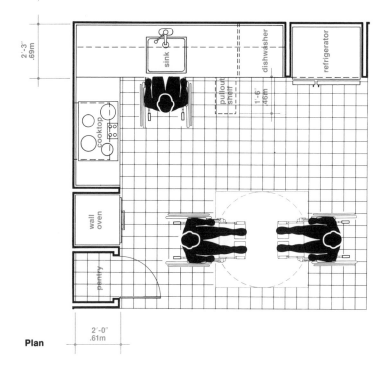

Plan

cm is best for the chairbound and is also convenient for others. No space should be allowed underneath the cooktop for the legs of a seated person because of the danger of hot spills. A lip along the front edge of the cooktop or a slot with a drain pan below it also reduce the danger from spilled hot liquid and food.

Storage Space
As with the side-by-side refrigerator, full-height storage space provides more accessibility for the disabled than the usual counter and cabinet arrangements. The middle space can be used by both the ambulant and the chairbound disabled while the high and low spaces can be used by either one or the other.

1. Wall oven, for easy access, open at counter height

2. Cooktop controls at the front, to avoid burning

3. Cooktop and counter, 30″/76 cm to 33″/84 cm height

4. Knee space under sink counter to allow sitting in wheelchair at counter

5. High recessed base under cabinets to accommodate wheelchair pedals

6. Pullout work shelf, 30″/76 cm to 33″/84 cm at standard height counters

7. Mixing faucet at sink, lever handle

8. Cove lighting under wall cabinets, bulb replacement within reach range

9. Shallow shelf over sink counter within reach range

10. Wall space within reach over sink counter, used for hanging utensils

11. Front-loading dishwasher

12. Side-by-side refrigerator doors to allow access to refrigerator and freezer

13. Full height storage closet for easy access

14. Cabinet space under wall oven within reach range

15. Drawers under cooktop and counter for easier access

16. Easy grip cabinet door pulls

17. High cabinets (out of reach for the chairbound) for other users

18. Smooth, nonskid flooring, open spaces for wheelchair passage

19. Round table to avoid corners, legs, or pedestal base with no apron to allow for wheelchair

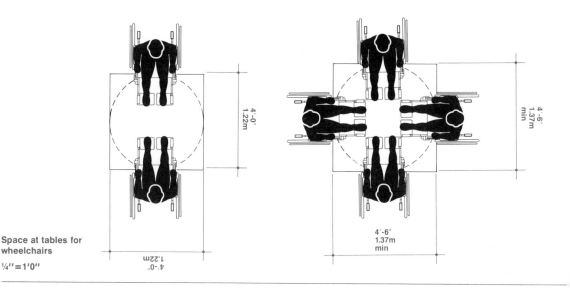

Space at tables for wheelchairs

¼″=1′0″

Dining Space

Space should be available for meals to be eaten in the kitchen or in a dining area readily accessible to the kitchen. The table should have clear leg space and no apron. This can be a table with pedestal supports or with widely spaced legs. If more than one person in a wheelchair is to sit at the table, the table should be wide enough to accommodate wheelchairs opposite each other.

These considerations are, of course, also applicable when planning restaurants or other dining spaces. There should be enough space around the perimeter of the tables and nearby furniture as well as the walls for comfortable wheelchair passage.

Comparison Chart in Inches

Comparison Chart Key, pages 64–65

		1 ANS	2 HUD	3 BSCP	4 NC	5 CCC	6 NYS	7 MICH	8 ME	9 VA	10 FAC	11 MASS	12 INT	13 LIST	14 BWB
1.	*Wheelchair dimensions*														
	a. length	42	ns	ns	42	ns	ns	ns	ns	ns	ns	48	42½	42	42
	b. open width	25	ns	ns	27	ns	ns	ns	ns	ns	ns	28	25	25	26
	c. collapsed width	11	ns	ns	11	ns	ns	ns	ns	ns	ns	13½	11	ns	13½
	d. seat to floor	19½	ns	ns	19½	ns	ns	ns	ns	ns	ns	19½	19½	16½	19½
	e. armrest to floor	29	ns	ns	29	ns	ns	ns	ns	ns	ns	29½	29	29	29
2.	*Parking stalls*														
	a. minimum width	144	ns	ns	150	144	120	144	ns	162	108	144	144	144	144
3.	*Curb cuts*														
	a. maximum slope	ns	ns	ns	ns	1:12	ns	1:3	ns	1:12	ns	1:12	ns	1:12	1:12
4.	*Public walks*														
	a. minimum width	48	48	ns	48	60	48	60	48	72	ns	48	48	48	60
	b. maximum slope	1:20	ns	ns	1:20	1:20	1:20	1:20	1:20	1:33	ns	1:20	1:20	1:20	1:20
5.	*Ramps*														
	a. minimum width	ns	ns	48	48	ns	48	36	ns	48	36	48	32	ns	36
	b. maximum slope	1:12	1:12	1:12	1:12	1:12	1:12	1:12	1:12	1:12	ns	1:12	ns	1:12	1:12
	c. unbroken length	360	ns	360	360	360	360	360	ns	ns	360	408	360	360	360
	d. handrail height	32	ns	36	32	33	32	32	32	ns	32	33	30–32	32	33
	e. handrail diameter	ns	ns	1¼–2	ns	ns	ns	ns	ns	ns	ns	1¼–2	ns	ns	1½
6.	*Platforms at doors*														
	a. door swing in	36x60	ns	48x48	60x60	ns	48 long	60x60	ns	60 long	ns	60x60	36x60	36x60	60 wide
	b. door swing out	60x60	ns	48x48	60x60	ns	48 long	60x60	ns	60 long	48 deep	60x72	60x60	60x60	60 wide
7.	*Entry doors*														
	a. minimum clear opening	32	36	31	32	32	32	32	32	40	32	34	36	32	34
	b. maximum pull	ns	ns	ns	8 lbs	ns	8 lbs	ns	ns	8 lbs	8 lbs	15 lbs	ns	ns	8 lbs
	c. handle height	ns	ns	42	ns	ns	42	ns	ns	36	42	36–42	36	ns	36
8.	*Stairs*														
	a. maximum riser height	7	7¾	6½	ns	ns	ns	7½	7	ns	7½	ns	ns	7	7
	b. maximum handrail height	32	ns	36	32	33	ns	32	32	ns	32	33	ns	32	33
	c. handrail diameter	ns	ns	ns	ns	ns	ns	ns	ns	ns	1½–2	1¼–2	ns	ns	1½
	d. handrails both sides?	yes	yes	yes	ns	ns	ns	ns	ns	yes	ns	yes	ns	yes	yes

		1 ANS	2 HUD	3 BSCP	4 NC	5 CCC	6 NYS	7 MICH	8 ME	9 VA	10 FAC	11 MASS	12 INT	13 LIST	14 BWB
9.	*Corridors*														
	a. minimum width	ns	60	48	42	ns	ns	48	ns	ns	60	ns	36	ns	48
	b. width for 90° turn	ns	ns	ns	60	ns	ns	60	ns	ns	ns	ns	54	ns	60
	c. width for 180° turn	ns	ns	ns	60	ns	ns	60	ns	ns	ns	ns	ns	ns	60
10.	*Elevators*														
	a. minimum dimensions	ns	ns	69x43	60x60	60x60	46 deep	60x60	ns	68x60	46x60	48x48	ns	*	68x51
	b. minimum door width	32	ns	ns	ns	36	32	32	ns	36	32	36	ns	ns	34
	c. maximum control height	ns	ns	54	48	55	60	60	ns	40	60	60	ns	48	60
	d. markings for the blind?	ns	ns	ns	yes	yes	ns	yes	yes	yes	ns	yes	ns	yes	yes
11.	*Public restrooms*														
	a. minimum toilet stall width	36	ns	54	36	42	36	48	ns	56/42	36	66	ns	36	36
	b. minimum toilet stall depth	60	ns	66	72	72	56	64	ns	72/78	66	72	ns	60	72
	c. grab bar height from floor	33	ns	11†	33	33	32	33	ns	30	32	33	8–10†	33	33
	d. toilet seat height	20	ns	20	20	19	19–20	ns	ns	15/20	19	18	16–20	ns	18
	e. washbasin height	ns	ns	ns	ns	ns	26	ns	ns	ns	ns	30	26	ns	31
	f. washbasin controls	ns	ns	lever	lever	lever/push button	wrist blade	ns	ns	lever/wrist blade	lever	ns	ns	ns	lever
	g. washbasin depth to wall	ns	ns	ns	ns	ns	ns	ns	ns	ns	ns	24	ns	ns	27
	h. mirror height	40	ns	ns	40	36	ns	40	ns	ns	36	40	31–69	40	40
	i. dispensers, shelves, disposal units height	40	ns	ns	40	40	ns	40	ns	40	ns	40	50½	40	40

* space for one wheelchair and one ambulant disabled person
† height from toilet seat

Comparison Chart in Centimeters

Comparison Chart Key, pages 64–65

		1 ANS	2 HUD	3 BSCP	4 NC	5 CCC	6 NYS	7 MICH	8 ME	9 VA	10 FAC	11 MASS	12 INT	13 LIS	14 BWB
1.	**Wheelchair dimensions**														
	a. length	107	ns	ns	107	ns	ns	ns	ns	ns	ns	122	108	107	107
	b. open width	63	ns	ns	69	ns	ns	ns	ns	ns	ns	71	63	63	66
	c. collapsed width	28	ns	ns	28	ns	ns	ns	ns	ns	ns	34	28	ns	34
	d. seat to floor	50	ns	ns	50	ns	ns	ns	ns	ns	ns	50	50	41	50
	e. armrest to floor	74	ns	ns	74	ns	ns	ns	ns	ns	ns	75	74	74	74
2.	**Parking stalls**														
	a. minimum width	366	ns	ns	381	366	305	366	ns	411	274	366	366	366	366
3.	**Curb cuts**														
	a. maximum slope	ns	ns	ns	ns	1:12	ns	1:3	ns	1:12	ns	1:12	ns	1:12	1:12
4.	**Public walks**														
	a. minimum width	122	122	ns	122	152	122	152	122	183	ns	122	122	122	152
	b. maximum slope	1:20	ns	ns	1:20	1:20	1:20	1:20	1:20	1:33	ns	1:20	1:20	1:20	1:20
5.	**Ramps**														
	a. minimum width	ns	ns	122	122	ns	122	91	ns	122	91	122	81	ns	91
	b. maximum slope	1:12	1:12	1:12	1:12	1:12	1:12	1:12	1:12	1:12	ns	1:12	ns	1:12	1:12
	c. unbroken length	915	ns	915	915	915	915	915	ns	ns	915	1036	915	915	915
	d. handrail height	81	ns	91	81	84	81	81	81	ns	81	84	76–81	81	84
	e. handrail diameter	ns	ns	3–5	ns	ns	ns	ns	ns	ns	ns	3–5	ns	ns	4
6.	**Platforms at doors**														
	a. door swing in	91x 152	ns	122x 122	152x 152	ns	122 long	152x 152	ns	152 long	ns	152x 152	91x 152	91x 152	152 wide
	b. door swing out	152x 152	ns	122x 122	152x 152	ns	122 long	152x 152	ns	152 long	122 deep	152x 183	152x 152	152 152	152x wide
7.	**Entry doors**														
	a. minimum clear opening	81	91	79	81	81	81	81	81	102	81	86	91	81	86
	b. maximum pull	ns	ns	ns	3.63kg	ns	3.63kg	ns	ns	3.63kg	3.63kg	6.80kg	ns	ns	3.63k
	c. handle height	ns	ns	107	ns	ns	107	ns	ns	91	107	91–107	91	ns	91
8.	**Stairs**														
	a. maximum riser height	18	20	17	ns	ns	ns	19	18	ns	19	ns	ns	18	18
	b. maximum handrail height	81	ns	91	81	84	ns	81	81	ns	81	84	ns	81	84
	c. handrail diameter	ns	ns	ns	ns	ns	ns	ns	ns	ns	4–5	3–5	ns	ns	4
	d. handrails both sides?	yes	yes	yes	ns	ns	ns	ns	ns	yes	ns	yes	ns	yes	yes

	1 ANS	2 HUD	3 BSCP	4 NC	5 CCC	6 NYS	7 MICH	8 ME	9 VA	10 FAC	11 MASS	12 INT	13 LIS	14 BWR
9. *Corridors*														
a. minimum width	ns	152	122	107	ns	ns	122	ns	ns	152	ns	91	ns	122
b. width for 90° turn	ns	ns	ns	152	ns	ns	152	ns	ns	ns	ns	137	ns	152
c. width for 180° turn	ns	ns	ns	152	ns	ns	152	ns	ns	ns	ns	ns	ns	152
10. *Elevators*														
a. minimum dimensions	ns	ns	175x 109	152x 152	152x 152	117 deep	152x 152		173x 152	117x 152	122x 122	ns	*	173x 130
b. minimum door width	81	ns	ns	ns	91	81	81	ns	91	81	91	ns	ns	86
c. maximum control height	ns	ns	137	122	140	152	152	ns	102	152	152	ns	122	152
d. markings for the blind?	ns	ns	ns	yes	yes	ns	yes	yes	yes	ns	yes	ns	yes	yes
11. *Public restrooms*														
a. minimum toilet stall width	91	ns	137	91	107	91	122	ns	142/ 107	91	168	ns	91	91
b. minimum toilet stall depth	152	ns	168	183	183	142	163	ns	183/ 195	168	183	ns	152	183
c. grab bar height from floor	84	ns	28†	84	84	81	84	ns	76	81	84	20– 25†	84	84
d. toilet seat height	51	ns	51	51	48	48– 51	ns	ns	38/ 51	48	46	41– 51	ns	46
e. washbasin height	ns	ns	ns	ns	ns	66	ns	ns	ns	ns	76	66	ns	79
f. washbasin controls	ns	ns	lever	lever	lever/ push button	wrist blade	ns	ns	lever/ wrist blade	lever	ns	ns	ns	lever
g. washbasin depth to wall	ns	ns	ns	ns	ns	ns	ns	ns	ns	ns	61	ns	ns	69
h. mirror height	102	ns	ns	102	91	ns	102	ns	ns	91	102	79– 175	102	102
i. dispensers, shelves, disposal units height	102	ns	ns	102	102	ns	102	ns	102	ns	102	128	102	102

* space for one wheelchair and one ambulant disabled person
† height from toilet seat

Comparison Chart Key

1
ANS
American National Standards Institute, Inc., *Specifications for Making Buildings and Facilities Accessible to, and Usable by, the Physically Handicapped.*

2
HUD
United States Department of Housing and Urban Development, *Minimum Property Standards for Multifamily Housing.* (Covers many construction and systems items that are not included in the chart.)

3
BSCP
The Council for Codes of Practice, British Standards Institution, *British Standard Code of Practice, Access for the Disabled to Buildings, Part I: General Recommendations.*

4
NC
Ronald L. Mace; Betsy Laslett, ed., *An Illustrated Handbook of the Handicapped Section of the North Carolina State Building Code.*

5
CCC
State of California, *Amendment to California Civil Code General Rules, Part 4. Amendment to Building Code,* Draft # 1.

6
NYS
State of New York, *Amendments to the State Building Construction Code Relating to Facilities for the Physically Handicapped.*

7
MICH
State of Michigan, Department of Management and Budget, Construction Division, *Making Facilities Accessible for the Handicapped, Rules Applying to and Act No. 1 of the Public Acts of 1966 and Act No. 243 of the Public Acts of 1970.*

8
ME
State of Maine, *Part 7, Public Buildings, Chapter 331, Construction for Physically Handicapped.*

9
VA
Veterans Administration, *Accommodations for the Physically Handicapped, VA Construction Standard CD-28, H-08-3.*

10
FAC
New York State University Construction Fund, *Making Facilities Accessible to the Physically Handicapped.*

11
MASS
The Commonwealth of Massachusetts
Department of Public Safety, *Rules and
Regulations of the Architectural Barriers
Board, Form ABR-1.*

12
INT
Sharon C. Olson and Diane K. Meredith,
Wheelchair Interiors.

13
LIST
State of California, prepared by John C.
Worsley, AIA, State Architect, *Check List
and Graphic Illustrations.*

14
BWB
Sarah P. Harkness and James N. Groom,
Jr., *Building without Barriers for the Dis-
abled.*

Feet	Meters
0	0.00000
1	0.30480
2	0.60960
3	0.91440
4	1.21920
5	1.52400
6	1.82880
7	2.13360
8	2.43840
9	2.74321
10	3.04801
1	3.35281
2	3.65761
3	3.96241
4	4.26721
5	4.57201
6	4.87681
7	5.18161
8	5.48641
9	5.79121
20	6.09601
1	6.40081
2	6.70561
3	7.01041
4	7.31521
5	7.62002
6	7.92482
7	8.22962
8	8.53442
9	8.83922
30	9.14402
1	9.44882
2	9.75362
3	10.05842
4	10.36322
5	10.66802
6	10.97282
7	11.27762
8	11.58242
9	11.88722
40	12.19202
1	12.49682
2	12.80163
3	13.10643
4	13.41123
5	13.71603
6	14.02083
7	14.32563
8	14.63043
9	14.93523
50	15.24003

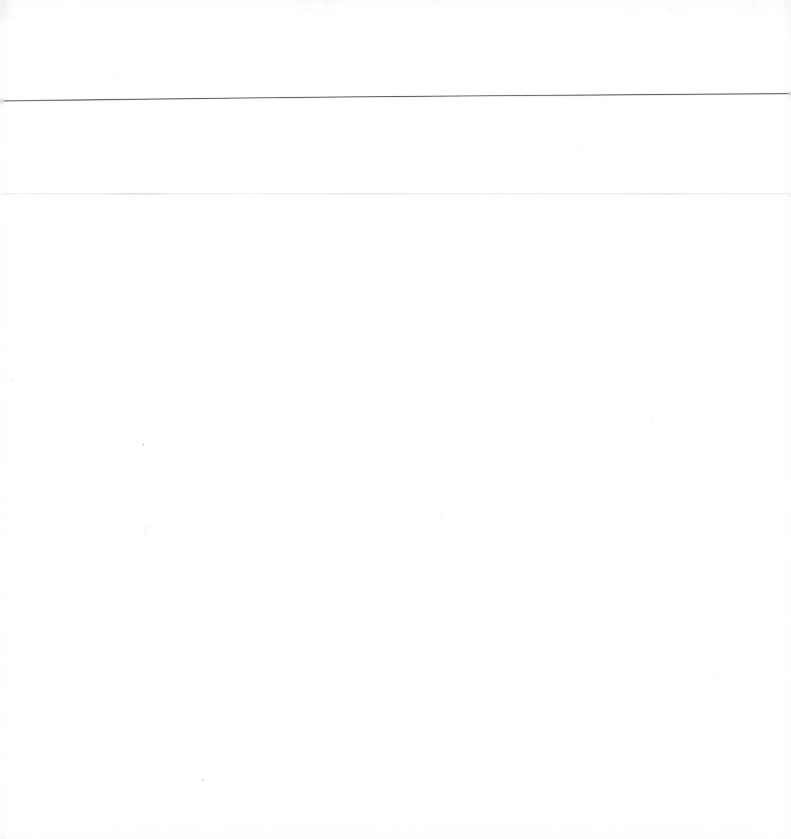

Amendment to California Civil Code General Rules, Part 4. Amendment to Building Code, Draft No. 1. Jan. 30, 1974.

American National Standards Institute, Inc. *Specifications for Making Buildings and Facilities Accessible to, and Usable by, the Physically Handicapped.* **New York, approved Oct. 31, 1961.**

The pioneer standard for this country. Most subsequent state and federal codes and regulations owe a heavy debt to this work. Deals mainly with public buildings.

Brattgard, Sven-Olof; Carlson, Folke; and Sandin, Arne. *Housing and Service for the Handicapped in Sweden.* **Goteborg: the Fokus Society, 1972.**

A description of the Fokus Society and its objectives, organization, and planning principles. Includes suggested apartment plans, kitchen and bathroom perspectives.

British Columbia. Department of Health Services and Hospital Insurance. *Hospitals for Extended Care: A Program and Design Guide.* **1st ed. Victoria, British Columbia, 1969.**

Most interesting is a full-scale mock-up of a toilet with a swing-away grab bar.

British Standards Institution. The Council for Codes of Practice. *British Standard Code of Practice. Access for the Disabled to Buildings. Part I: General Recommendations.* **London, 1967.**

Commonwealth of Massachusetts. Department of Public Safety. *Rules and Regulations of the Architectural Barriers Board, Form ABR-1.* **Boston, June 10, 1975.**

A very stringent code based on feedback from an earlier version. It is very complete, with sections devoted to different building types.

Diffrient, Niels; Tilley, Alvin R.; and Bardagiy, Joan C. *Humanscale 1/2/3.* **Designer: Henry Dreyfuss Associates. Cambridge, Massachusetts: MIT Press, 1974.**

Three illustrated plastic cards, one of which is for the chairbound and ambulant disabled. A revolving wheel on the card shows measurements for men, women, and children of different ages and sizes.

Easter Seal Society for Crippled Children and Adults of Massachusetts, Inc. in cooperation with United Community Planning Corporation. *Access 76.* **Boston, 1975.**

The Fokus Society. *Principles of the Fokus Housing Units for the Severely Disabled.* **Prepared by a research group at the request of the Fokus Society. February 1968. Re-edited December 1969.**

An excellent reference going into great detail. Many of the recommendations may only be possible in a socially oriented country like Sweden, but they are something for the United States to strive for. One of the best recommendations we have seen.

Goldsmith, Selwyn. *Designing for the Disabled.* **2d ed. London: Royal Institute of British Architects, 1967.**

In a class by itself as a reference for architects interested in a detailed study of designing for the handicapped. Many illustrations and anthropometric drawings. Many of the recommendations are best suited to England; many solutions use products not readily available in the United States. However, the principles are valid.

Goldsmith, Selwyn. "Wheelchair Housing." Section 7 contributed by Janis Morton. *The Architects Journal,* **June 25, 1975, pp. 1319–1348.**

Hillery, J. F. "Buildings for All to Use." *AIA Journal,* **March 1969, pp. 41–48. Annotated bibliography, pp. 40, 50, 82, 84.**

Very clear illustrations showing basic requirements in public buildings.

Kidwell, Ann Middleton; and Greer, Peter Swartz. *Sites Perception, and the Nonvisual Experience.* **Published by the American Foundation for the Blind. Montpelier: Capital City Press, 1973.**

Discusses the development of maps which help the blind find their way.

Kliment, Stephen A. *Into the Mainstream: A Syllabus for a Barrier-Free Environment.* **Prepared under a grant to the American Institute of Architects by the Rehabilitation Services Administration of the Department of Health, Education, and Welfare. June 1975.**

A general overview of the state of the art from legislative and policy matters to design recommendations and bibliography.

Mace, Ronald L. *An Illustrated Handbook of the Handicapped Section of the North Carolina State Building Code.* **Edited by Betsy Laslett. Raleigh: North Carolina Building Code Council and North Carolina Department of Insurance, 1974.**

A comprehensive state code with detailed, clear illustrations.

National Swedish Building Research Institute. *Accessible Towns—Workable Homes.* **Stockholm, 1972.**

Divided into two parts. The first part deals with the scale of the urban environment. The second part deals with standard dwellings including sanitary facilities, sleeping accommodations, dining areas, and service areas for washing, drying, ironing, etc.

New York State University Construction Fund. *Making Facilities Accessible to the Physically Handicapped.* **Albany, 1974.**

Oriented to campus problems but very helpful and clearly illustrated for general use. Covers exterior and interior problem area. Tells "what to do" very well, but not much explanation of "why."

Olson, Sharon C.; and Meredith, Diane K. *Wheelchair Interiors.* Chicago: National Easter Seal Society for Crippled Children and Adults, 1973.

Illustrated with photographs. Shows detailed arrangements for the disabled in kitchen, laundry, bathroom, and bedroom.

Ries, Michael L. *Design Standards to Accommodate People with Physical Disabilities in Park and Open Space Planning.* Madison: Recreation Resources Center, University of Wisconsin Extension, 1973.

A manual of recommendations for modifying park and open space design allowing an increase in the recreational potential for people with physical disabilities.

State of Maine. *An Act Requiring Constructed Public Buildings Be Made Accessible to the Physically Handicapped. H.P. 1114–L.D. 1583. Part 7. Public Buildings: Chapter 331. Construction for Physically Handicapped.* 1967 and *S.P. 100–L.D. 310.* 1969.

State of Maine. *An Act Requiring the Ramping of Curbs at Crosswalks for Physically Handicapped and Elderly Persons. S.P. 585–L.D. 1797.* 1973.

State of Michigan. Department of Management and Budget. Construction Division. *Making Facilities Accessible for the Handicapped. Rules Applying to and Act No. 1 of the Public Acts of 1966 and Act No. 243 of the Public Acts of 1970.* Reissued February 1974.

State of New York. Housing and Building Codes Bureau. *Amendments to the State Building Construction Code Relating to Facilities for the Physically Handicapped.* New York, Jan. 1, 1971.

United States Department of Health, Education, and Welfare. *Technical Handbook for Facilities Engineering and Construction Manual. Section 4.12: Design of Barrier-Free Facilities.* Washington, D.C., 1974.

United States Department of Housing and Urban Development. *Minimum Property Standards for Multifamily Housing.* Washington, D.C., 1973.

University of Edinburgh. Department of Urban Design and Regional Planning. *Planning for Disabled People in the Urban Environment.* London: Central Council for the Disabled, 1969.

Includes twelve case studies with summary and visits to selected urban centers in England with analysis from the point of view of a disabled user. Gives conclusions and recommendations. Deals on an urban scale; does not get into details.

Veterans Administration. *Accommodations for the Physically Handicapped. VA Construction Standard CD-28, H-08-3.* **Washington, D.C., 1973.**

Worsley, John C. *Check List and Graphic Illustrations.* **California Council, American Institute of Architects, San Francisco.**

Developed for use as a guide in designing state-funded buildings and facilities to ensure compliance with the "Physically Handicapped Law."

The authors wish to express their appreciation to the following members of The Architects Collaborative Inc. who contributed to the book: editorial contributions, Katherine Selfridge, Martha Bertrand; graphic design, Valerie Pettis, April Greiman; photography, Pamela Webster; illustrations, Bruce Owensby, Victor Hagen, Dennis Brady; perspective drawings, Branko Petrovic.

Additional credits for photography are: photo 1, Samuel Ross; photo 2, Mark PoKempner; illustrations 26-31, Ronald Mace.